SHADOWS
OF
TIME

To my family

SHADOWS
OF
TIME

POEMS BY

HAIG
KHATCHADOURIAN

WIPF & STOCK · Eugene, Oregon

Wipf and Stock Publishers
199 W 8th Ave, Suite 3
Eugene, OR 97401

Shadows of Time
By Khatchadourian, Haig A.
Copyright©1983 by Khatchadourian, Haig A.
ISBN 13: 978-1-60899-816-6
Publication date 7/7/2010
Previously published by Ashod Press, 1983

CONTENTS

We *are the moving shadows of time*
ephemeral, frail
cast on the surface of nothingness
by the long cold rays of eternity

With the exception of "In Memory of My Mother," all the poems in this volume have been previously published, and are reprinted with the kind permission of the magazines in which they appeared. Acknowledgment is made to *Quest* in which "Rain on the Pond" originally appeared; to *Volume 63* in which "Shy Eyes Shy Looks" originally appeared; and to *Ararat* for the rest of the poems.

I

PROEM

I have long waited for the hour of glory;
when the sharp lightning of thought shall smite
the dull brain, the shiver blanch the cheek
and speed along the bone.
But the spasm lingers yet, the lightning
has yet to fall; and I,
like a beggar at a rich man's door,
must still collect the crusts of thought,
the crumbs of song.

WATER COLOR

it is a still morning in March;
and yet the last traces of rain have gone from
    the sky
and no traditional dew drops hang on the lilac
    flowers.
but winter is still in the air
with an anachronism of smell of flowers and gras
and lingers in the humid bough,
and looms faint pink
in the snows of Lebanon.
a tiny boat slides upon the polished sea
with tiny oars churning the streaming light.
below, a cart rumbles along:
(an element of asymmetry in the Still Life,
an element of movement;
an intrusion of the individual upon the eternal:
impertinent, unique;
a thread of laughter in a brocade of song).

WATER COLOR II

evening.
the wispy clouds are crowded round the sun
tinted with prismatic colors:
drifting islands in a waveless ocean,
or feathery canopies built on air.
the light withdraws from earth, air and sea;
the day wanes slowly toward the eclipse of night;
the present moment dissolves to shadows blurred
        and far away,
touched with the quality of dreams.
a bird rehearses a few last notes.
a few wings flutter.
the pulse of things beats slower
and the swift blood is quieted.

exhaled by the sea they curl up into snow
skyspume or burnished icicles of light
and hang from the blue cornice of the air gay
forms of the everchanging hours.
such airy grandeur, such soaring bulk
such cloudy architecture tease the mind
and from the massive marble of the clouds
rise mansions roofed and walled with light
great halls with colonnades of opal and spar
chambers for the dwelling of winds spires
pinnacles towers buttressed by air
and gargoyles crawling and soaring things solem
    saints
sculptured by the wind.

such lofty structures are not solider than air:
they thaw, dissolve, or crumble into rain
or drift across the stream of air
like floating weeds, to another sky;
or lift their anchors and set sail:
like life that crumbles into tears,
like dreams that do not stay.

SEASCAPE: WOMAN ON THE BEACH

like little suns snared by twilight waves
are her eyes, like lights
harbored at night in a summer bay;
and her hair is like the shadows
of seagulls' wings on the waves.

the white curve of her back and flank
is like the curve of the seacoast
white with foam.

her breasts are like seagulls rising
against the sky of her bosom.

sprawling, forgotten at her side lie her arms
like freckled seaweeds abandoned on the lagging
    shore.

her thighs are like white rocks of the bay
smoothed by the sea's bluegreen hands.

and the dreams in her little soul
are like a shaft of white light falling
on the deep, cold, dark, shellstrewn ocean floor.

RAIN ON THE POND

(allegro moderato)

endless
beads of rain-drops
plummet placidly
pearl-like, pure heaven dew,
upon the pond's elastic surface,
patting the water with long liquid fingers,
expanding in circle-within-circle of little ripples
like opening water-lilies or lotus flowers blooming
multiplying in concentric circles, ever-larger circle:
intersect . . . spread out . . . farther . . . lightly-tra
    lace-like delicate
like life's ripples . . . traced . . . on . . . time's wa
larger . . . fainter . . . farther . . . scarcely percept
    over . . .

(presto)

slender
strings of rain-drops
pat the water with long liquid fingers
with the sound of syncopated pattering of many pi
running *staccato molto allegro vivace* in demisemiqu
    time . . .

THE COMING OF SNOW

I awoke one morning and the
sudden snow was there, white
in a world of grey, right to our door,
piled up in silence between midnight and dawn.

the wolfish wind prowled fiercely about
howling its ire at the anaemic sky, biting
the leafshorn boughs of maple trees
locusts and pines, sniffing the stinging snow.

there was no place for early snow
in our calendar, made only
for the deceitful rain and morning frost;
we shivered enough without the snow.

but as it came, sudden and stinging
it was heart-warming to sit behind the panes
near the defensive fire, and feel at home;
as when, long ago
it stirred up in the wondering boy
a strange feeling of home when
huddled behind a shuttered window, he
watched the snow's white hosts invade the world.

A POEM IS AN ORGANIC THING

a poem is an organic thing
like flesh or feathers, or the core
of august apples ripening from within.

like apples it only thrives
in the hosannah of light and warmth,
enfolded by life, rooted in
the genial human soil.

it is also like a crystal;
a little octagon of thought
that suddenly grows arboreal
from the saturated mind,

or like a lambent pearl, secreted
under the mind's oceanic tides
unseen, round a sandgrain
of wounding joy, or brittle pain.

or, to change the simile,
it is like a lark's song
that breaks upon the ear, suddenly,
when we are all alone with
evening and the round horizon, from a
sentinel tree, in fields hushed with corn,

and leaves a trill in the memory
that lasts long after it is gone,

like still dreamscenes of long ago
we sometimes halfremember,
quite uncertain if they are
inhabitants of our dingy world
or of the distant universe of desire.

II

LOVE POEM

sleep, love, in the long night,
strong in the haven of my arms,
oblivious of death that must come at last.
I know my love cannot keep death away:
it slips through love's fingers like the fluid years;
the moments burn in your unshielded flesh
with maiming flame, and the great flare
of youth flickers down to the ash's final grave.
life and the world, too, mock lovers' pains,
their argent vows, their wide-eyed visions;
the heart wears out, or the spirit wearies:
whatever is noble is quick to decay.
yet while love lasts, death is for us
diminished shadows on a gleaming peak;
a ripple on still waters;
a poor phantom-dream
stalking along the battlements of thought,
banished by the sudden day of sight.

In Remembrance

now that our parting is an accomplished fact
and time is an uphill road that I must climb
with the length of years, to meet you on the other
I must remember you now and again
almost casually, almost as a name;
I must school my heart not to yearn for you,
not to think of you with sudden pain.

I must think of you only as someone I've met
casually on a bus, on the busy street,
nodded politely to, or exchanged a few
inconsequential words as "How do you do?"
all our united past must be laid away
very carefully, like old porcelain,
to be gazed at wistfully once in a while
but not to be caressed or to be touched;
like china too precious to be used
even on holidays.

but when, at last, we meet again on the other side
of the summit of years, I shall throw aside
the reserve of my heart, shall open wide
the cupboard-doors, and take out the past;
the common past turned to common present
while we've been thinking we were far apart.

YOU SEEMED SO POISED AND TENDER TONIGHT

you seemed so poised and tender
tonight, so serene
in the charmed circle of my arms;
resplendent in your woman's love,
untouched by the stains of time.

the white flame of your kisses scorched my lips
your hands tore a tempest from my breast.
your fertile limbs were a honeycomb
of summer nights heavy with scent, infused
with the stars' amber glint . . .

then our wedded bodies lay still.
the waves of feeling racing
through our turbulent flesh receded, sank like the spent
ocean at low tide. a luminous
calm wove its magic charm
round us, like a runic spell.
time trickled past or even
seemed to stop.

but suddenly from the foliaged shadows
of that lull a slimy doubt crept
with cunning insinuation into
the eden of my happiness:
with eyeless pain
I groped for you beside me
for the solid comfort of touch. yet even as
your swooning flesh revived under my grip
I sadly knew that you were far away

in a world from which even I was barred,
burgeoning behind the locked gates of
your forehead (adorned with innocent hair
I touch and caress); and I was helpless
to guess what your inner eye was
gazing at and I unable to see.

and as I wondered,
a sudden thought, like a midnight flare
lit up the ghostly landscape of my brain:
I was now aware
that you too (perhaps)
were thinking the same thought as I and,
like me, searching, with nothing but fingertips,
lips and arms for a guide,
for the essential self that lay disguised
in the clumsy disarray of bare breast and arms

THE LONG WAITING

when you come
I shall be ready
with my sunday soul
to take you in

my soul shall go out to embrace you
with extended arms

it takes long to be ready
to sweep the soul clean
burnish the furniture
pull up the blinds
to let the morning in

it takes a lifetime to be ready
and perhaps more than a lifetime
and perhaps more than that too

so I shall wait
I shall not be impatient
and cry for you before your time
and stamp my feet
and sigh like a loverchild
it is never a waste of soul to wait
for one who will come at last

my waiting shall be illuminated by you
as the dawn is by the invisible sun
time will pass
with the speed of lovers' looks—

and what time does not pass!
my time shall be redeemed
with thoughts sweetened by you.

and waiting and weariness
shall be forgotten
and the past shall not matter
when you arrive

but if I am ready
after long years
to meet you
with my sunday soul
to take you in
and you do not hear me?

and my words beat the air
sadly, vainly, in despair?

if you do not see me?

if I wait and you never come near me?

III

SHY EYES SHY LOOKS

shy eyes shy looks meet
on timehunched bridges
in restaurants buses subways
on the corners of nameless streets
and kiss
embrace
caress
(discreetly slyly)
blue green
black brown

girlocks goldlocks
brush
bodies lightly touch

tentative smiles
like silk ribbons
float past

a few halfcrushed words
are thrown like crumpled
paper into the silent
arena of their minds

pupils press uncertainly through
the breach in the botched wall
from the tunnel
dug with the bare hands
into the other's soul

or fingers grope in the bateyed cave
of otherness just stumbled into
with nightblindness still
in the eyes

then they draw apart

grow remote again

indifferent preoccupied

no longer enticed
by the neophyte vision
of the essential man
under the mobile mask

like drunks
in crowing hours
swaying in the manblotted streets
they stumble away
from the newfound dawn

without a whisper a nod
a look behind
they sink
dissolve
in the eddied
turbulent crowd

NOCTURN FOR A WINTER NIGHT

the wind whips the world's offal across the streets
with the crackle of a consumptive's cough,
spraying me with sputum from the sky.
the dirty light lies in puddles at my feet.
the mad moon beats a tattoo, like a drum.
january cats scream in heat
as I tramp in the anaemic streets.

the rotting pavements rock under my vacant step,
mocking, mocking in the halflight
under a truncated moon.
my mind is a skeletal street
where only cats scream, lonely in desire.

young and old sleep with their
limp lovers interred in their arms;
or drugged with dreams mimicking their despair.
but some, sleepless like me,
cringe behind the refuge of their cells
and hear the echoes of my feet
vibrate within the cranium of their woes.

I swagger in the january alleys of life
where midnight minions squirm in mockdesire.
my brain and legs reel, like the double moon;
drunk with a flaming, stabbing wine.

THE FEAST

the feast was ready but nobody came
the chairs remained empty the cups without wine
the candles on the table burned in solitude
the wealth of foods remained untouched
and I sat there alone waiting
for my loved ones that would not come

I waited expectant till it seemed it was vain to exp
(counting the plates and the host of shadowy crock
moulded by candlelight nodding like a proper host
to the guests in the empty chairs half smiling in fa
to an apt joke made across the table
half framing an apter reply)
till the candles burnt low till it seemed
the hours stopped till I was left in darkness

then I fell to the food set before me
and feasted on the dainties prepared for my guests
I had offered my soul to my loved ones to feast on
but they spurned my feast and stayed away
I raised my arm in the empty air
and drank a toast to the clinking of empty cups
to empty chairs
I drank of all the cups in turn I emptied all the wi
till I was drunk with my own self
till my head reeled till my heart ached with surfeit

till I wept with drunken laughter
till I laughed with maddened sobbing
that none of my loved ones had come to my feast

SUFFERING DOES NOT ENNOBLE

suffering does not ennoble
or purge, except of folly.
the sufferer bites evil
to the bitter core,
knows the mirage
in the oasis of the soul.
anatomist in pain
dissects ague to the bone.
he knows how to be alone.
he knows how to atone.

WE LIVE ALONE

we live alone
whether together or apart

whether shuttling about
in the Undergrounds of time
rushing from station
to station with the miming crowd
whether caught
in the silver noose
of each other's laughter
or held captive
in each other's arms

whether together or apart
we are alone
in separate cells
of delinquent desires
scribbling our despair
on the dirty walls
enacting violent dreams
of escape or release
hoarding blunted hopes
like bits of broken saws

we stay apart; we too
o my love; but
in our apartness, I and you,
our fingertips, like
torches of pinewood, touch
a moment (mortals call
it love); we manage
(we do) to speak together
a little word or two.

DEAD SEA

everlasting symbol of negation in the universe element
    nonbeing
negative copula in life's logic divorce of essence and
    existence
we invoke you spirit of death slow sedate
    sulphurous mocking our sweat
by your sterile shores

we have drunk of your bitter waters bathed in your salt
we have slept by your silent waves under the hot moon
and saw your leaden surface shimmer like the surface o
    unreality

unreal sea! mysterious hermetic sea
solitary remote like the hairy Essenes
who on your sand spelt out a religion of dearth and
    solitude
vast mirage trapping the eye in the sands of the desert

the language of your waves is the utterance of the deaf
slow muffled painful halfsecret scarce audible
intelligible only to the sands and the salty rocks
and the mountains squatting by your side like huge ston
    hounds
keeping watch or gazing at their image in your opaque
    eyes
in eternal selflove

no slimy moss or weed has been nourished by your
    water sea of death
not a fin has fluttered in it not a dissolved bubble of air
has been inhaled by a living lung
your waters tumble on a sediment of powdered skulls
    and dessicated glory of sin
at the bottom of death

John the thunderer did not baptize in your lethal waters
those who sought life but who or what there is
can ever escape its final dip of death?
strange thought—that the waters of the Font
in which the messenger of eternal life baptized even Him
sink down to you dead sea!

ELEGY

you are not here in this puerile grave.
all that was you is not resigned to dust
fast food for worms. what you are now
is what we kept of you: a pinch
of arid images scattered in a dozen minds.
let the worm triumph over your flesh;
it triumphs and you are not defeated:
what is your flesh, now that you're cleansed of f
and yet, why do I linger?—I *know*
you are not here . . . But when,
sometimes, I think of what you were:
beauty and grace and light and fire—
your image in my mind is poor effigy of you—
I foolishly come here, hoping to find you.

IN MEMORY OF DR. MARTIN LUTHER KING*

I   all of us died with you
      in memphis tennessee
      we were buried in your grave
      in atlanta georgia

II   we were burned and baptized in your blood
      in memphis tennessee
      because we too would rather die
      than live as another's slave

III   you were the nobler part of ourselves
      felled but shall rise again

IV   mankind's newly-wakened conscience crying
      in the cottonfields of hate
      in a mad world whirling about

V   on merrygorounds of lusts
      while the hunted the outcasts
      scrounge in slums
      for discarded crusts of love

VI   yet we are all your murderers
      (in memphis tennessee)
      with our bloodied hands
      we drove the nails
      into your unresisting flesh

VII   you who taught so well
       in georgia washington d.c.
       that loneliness and pain
       do not discriminate

VIII   that despair and death
       are fully integrated
       (in atlanta georgia
       in memphis tennessee)

IX   you had a dream that will not die
       (in memphis tennessee)
       but like a sun shall blossom
       from mississippi to capetown

X   or spread like the mighty oak
       in whose shade abraham sat
       blessed with the nearness of god
       a tree with a million branches outstretch
       and a million young leaves on each

XI   then love will triumph
       in london moscow budapest
       and memphis tennessee

XII   then man- and woman-kind
       will stand as one
       garlanded in deathless light

XIII   united in perfect equality

XIV   *epitaph*
        here lies a man
        his giant faith transformed
        nights of despair to dawns of hope
        carved out of a people's pain
        towering fortresses of the spirit
        a knight whose armor was
        the untarnished steel of justice
        his sword the tempered edge of truth
        a soldier of peace who never faltered
        who rose with every fall
        a hero of faith
        whose life taught us how to live
        whose death taught us how to die

* The fourteen stanzas—marked for emphasis with Roman numerals—
symbolize the fourteen Stations of the Cross

IN MEMORY OF MY MOTHER (1908-19

To be performed by a Solemn Chorus
dynamics *ad libitum*

I.

First Voice: in death
                    lies peace
                    in
                       death
                       lies
                             peace

Second Voice: lie
                    in
                    death
                    in
                    peace
                    lie

Third Voice: lie
                    death
                    lie

                    peace
                    lies
                    in death

                    peace
                    in death
                    LIES

Chorus: in peace in

death in lies
lies lies lies
death death death
peace peace peace

II.

First Voice: after death
                 lies

Second Voice: life after
                 death

Third Voice: death
                 life

First Voice: life after death
                     after death
                         lies   lies

Second Voice: here and after
                 hereafter
                 after death
                 what   what   after

Chorus: nothing
                     nothing
                     nothing

                     end of all
                     all end
                     nothing

III.

Third Voice: what

      peace   after death

                lies

      peace

               all nothing

           what

               all   to

                      nothing

First Voice: what

      for

      nothing

      nothing

Second Voice: all that

      nothing

        for that

        nothing

        for

        nothing

           all

           all

        nothing

IV.

Third Voice: for

      suffering

                    nothing
                    for

First Voice: senseless
                        nothing
                    suffering
                        nothing
                    suffering suffering
                        senseless

Second Voice: less sense
                            sense less
                        yes sense less
                            less suffering

Chorus: suffering
                    nothing
                    death
                    peace
                    in death
                    less sense less
                    not senseless
                    what
                    life   not
                                senseless
                                suffering

                            what

                    not

IV

IN THE PRESENT WE TAKE REFUGE FROM THE PAST

in the present we take refuge from the past
in the future we take refuge from the present
in the intellect we take refuge from the heart.
but refuge in the future is hope
and hope is of the heart
which is a bridge between the present and future
and leads back to the past.
the alleys of time meander to the past
which lives in the heart as the marrow of the future
as the sap of the present.
and past, present and future dwell together in the heart.

the intellect comprehends the past only
as grave, as epitaph, only as the bloodstained point
where time is murdered. The hungry heart's seasurge
    between yesterday and today
it does not heed, or sees only as mad play.

but I must return to the past
that I may cleanse myself of its pollution
and also that I may wash myself in its renewing waters.
I must return to the past's womb to be reborn.
I am the offspring of my past and
must be suckled at its breast.

the memory of unhappiness and
the memory of happiness—both are
painful.

JERUSALEM

you are the dreams we sadly leave behind—
and we must all someday part from our darling d
as the wide and smooth thoroughfares of childhoo
    dwindle
to the narrow graveled paths of youth and age,
but now and then, from the refracted distance
turn back our astigmatic gaze upon
as something familiar, yet grown
strange like an old face encountered
after long years. the sudden shock that something
has been lost, never to be retrieved, tempers
the joy of recognition; we feel that something
torn from ourselves
has been bartered away for mere baubles.
they are like milestones of our decline,
marking the points where we betrayed ourselves
or let the world betray us.

In a Minor Key

I have wagered the certain present for an uncertain
    future
gambled away the pressing pleasure for a distant
    glory

I have spurned the senses' sleek softness
the velvet of the moistened palate
the thrill of naked flesh
the largeness of free exercise of limbs

I have waited with tightened sinews in brooding and
    solitariness
practicing religiousness of soul asceticism of body
in secrecy and silence I've heard and seen and
    pondered
and stored for the great day

miser for the morrow I have been prodigal of today
but today lengthened into a morrow and the morrow
    into another today
and still I wait and still I gamble away
with hope as my riches my diminishing gold

EACH OF US HERE HAS FOUGHT THIS BA

FOR C.S.

each of us here has fought this battle,
bravely or cowardly, well or ill;
fought as best he could, as much as gun
could kill bayonet pierce and tear and spill
till strength snapped
surrendered or fell
in booby-traps in trenches on piles
of corpses or tore his flesh
on barbed-wire fences: the worst
of hell was over
and appeased the kite and the raven.

each of us here has fought alone
against dim forces he could not comprehend
in mist or rain, in darkness, marsh or fen, against
an enemy he did not meet face to face;
and what the gain he was not sure at all;
and if he won or lost he could not well decide;
and if the fight was worth it he could not ever say.

such a battle we fought—do not say
our fathers or forefathers were better combatants,
knew how and when and why to fight,
how to win, how to rejoice in victory:
the battle was the same, the battlefield one;
only we are changed, only the weapons old-fashionec
　　new. they too

knew the bitterness of surrender, the fall,
the blade in the flesh, the war-song
of the foe; and the emptiness of it all,
even of victory, when the first dawn of joy
ripens into surfeit. they too
felt the hot flame of tears furrow their cheeks; they too
mourned for the precious things that were so trite.

you who know our failings do not judge
by what we did but what we tried to do;
how high we shot; what we have shunned;
what we have paid as price—
do not judge harshly; for in our different ways
we had a common aim, and our dank doom is the same.

traffic with time is a terrible thing.
fire burns less than time burns flesh.
daggers are blunt as seconds are sharp,
cut into our being and bleed the spirit.

and I, trafficker with time between past and future,
scatter my life between morning and night.
walking along the shore I watch the ships
dip into the horizon of the nascent minute
and in the public squares see the hands of the clock
move like fingers on Belshazzar's wall.

                                    thus my life is crc
between the hour and the quarter strokes
of the clocks in obscure places;
at tea-time in the morning, at work time;
in the summer-afternoon nap, in the evening stroll b'
    sea;
in the laughter of summer evenings,
in the white silence of long winter nights.
and while I live I am murdered
with the whirling of metal cogs,
between the monotonous ticks of clocks.

but time that scavenges my defunct self
redeems me from my past:
the facetious fears and frets, the
ingenious regrets, the backward-turning gaze.
I am reborn with every moment's death.

thus every moment is also like a cross-road
where I must leave the well-known path
and take a new road. I cannot stop. I must
move on to another cross-road, to the
beginning of another road.

so every moment is also a new farewell, a
lifting of the anchor, a setting sail,
and a new kind of meeting before the journey's end.

and every moment
is an unravelling, an unwinding of tangled threads
of thought and feeling; a gradual lifting of the fog;
a gradual illumination; a simplification
and clarification of myself.

and so with gladness I shall climb the gangway
to the new moment, ready to embark
on a quest from which I shall not return
to the same pier on which I stand.
I must not stop, I must not
hesitate, I must not turn round.

V

EASTER

every man is betrayed at least once
with a kiss. every man is accused at least once
and judged by a Pilate. every man
is raised upon the cross of shame,
nailed with the nails of suffering, crowned
with the mock wreath of bitter achievement.
every man cries at least once in his life:
"Father, why hast thou forsaken me?"
every man's clothes are divided at least once by his
    benefactors,
by lot by his friends.
every man dies at least once
with men whose only bond with him is death:
every man has his Good Friday in life's seven days
and is interred in the grave of despair.
but happy is he, who, on the return of light,
when his Peter, on tiptoe, peers sadly into his grave,
sees the stone rolled off, empty the grave.
happy the man who triumphs over death
and rises transfigured on the third day.

SILENCE

silence has a power of communication
denied to sense. the ear has only one language,
one language the eye, the hands. silence
is seen, heard, felt, tasted and smelled.
it has a flowering body vivid as a rose
which the perceptive hands can explore, and rea
                                    every po
of that body proclaims its message
to the listening fingers; and the sensitive eyes
can feel it blossom like a rose.

the way of silence is the way of the pregnant so
the way of self-abnegation in a world loud and s
    proclaiming,
the way beyond the way of speech; that leads to
    knowledge and the wisdom
that it is vain to speak. thus silence
leads only to silence; and in that greater silence
the lesser is extinguished and fulfilled
like the star's light fulfilled in sunlight.
the way of silence is sad, solitary, secret,
long as the soul which it traverses,
hard and rocky as the soul, mountainous
and dusty and sinuous. but he
who walks that way will never meet
a blind alley, but always see
new scenes unfolding like petals of a rose;
nor will he need to turn his face, or return.

for there, perhaps, beyond the farthest stretches of the
    soul
something or someone may be awaiting him
in which all journeys end, which is
the beginning and termination of all roads.

ANGELUS

sometimes the scheming mind is hushed
like streets in a small suburban town
stilled by midnight. ambition and desire,
the obstinate pursuit of means and ends, the itch
to reach beyond the moment, are all gone;
only the heart is prayerful
and painful with fullness of itself
and aching with fullness of feeling
you wonder what, or how, or why.
the present moment grows and expands
like scenes unfolded by a receding mist
or like the spreading sun; gathering
into itself the future and the past
like the horizon embracing earth and sky.
a sense of gratitude pervades the heart
for all that life has given it
to keep and cherish, for the sights
and beauties of the world and the mystery
of intimate love; a sense of unity
with all things blessed with beauty;
and yet a sense of vast humility
toward all things;
as when in a field,
alone with earth and evening and the all-embracir
when wind whistles over tall wild grass
and pendulous trees shake their twilight boughs,
a sudden bird's trill from a thorny bush
startles you, quickening your blood, and deepens
the silence and the loneliness
of the encircling horizons lost in hazy distances.

this pause, this twilight-hush of heart may come
in the most unexpected places, at the most unexpected
    hours;
in subways, streets, buses, at the height of noon, in
    crowds.
the place and time are immaterial when it comes,
since then they *cease* to matter. for though
you may go on doing ordinary things
you will be doing nothing; and though
you are in crowds you'll be alone
(but not in the emptiness of loneliness)
and grateful to be alone. the self
draws a deep breath and holds it, wanting nothing,
thinking nothing; only standing still
in singing silence, being itself
to the brim of the overflowing soul.